Rock Climbing

BY MATT DOEDEN

AMICUS HIGH INTEREST • AMICUS INK

Amicus High Interest and Amicus Ink are imprints of Amicus
P.O. Box 1329, Mankato, MN 56002
www.amicuspublishing.us

Library of Congress Cataloging-in-Publication Data
Doeden, Matt.
 Rock climbing / by Matt Doeden.
    pages cm. – (Great outdoors)
Includes webography.
Includes bibliographical references and index.
 Summary: "This photo-illustrated book for elementary students
describes the sport of climbing. Includes information on safety,
equipment, and good mountains, hills, or cliff faces to try this
adventure sport"– Provided by publisher.
 Audience: Grade: K to Grade 3.
 ISBN 978-1-60753-801-1 (library binding : alk. paper)
 ISBN 978-1-68151-021-7 (ebook)
 ISBN 978-1-68152-080-3 (paperback : alk. paper)
 1. Rock climbing–Juvenile literature. I. Title.
 GV200.2.D64 2017
 796.522'3–dc23

                                   2015023966

Editor: Wendy Dieker
Series Designer: Kathleen Petelinsek
Book Designer: Tracy Myers
Photo Researcher: Rebecca Bernin

Photo Credits: Greg Epperson/Shutterstock cover; Don
Mason/Blend Images/Corbis 5; Ryan Creary/All Canada
Photos/Corbis 6; Ted Levine/Corbis 9; Inu/Shutterstock
10; Corey Rich/Aurora Open/Corbis 13; scotto72/iStock
14; Jeff Morgan 13/Alamy Stock Photo 17; Patrick Lane/
Somos Images/Corbis 18-19; Greg Epperson/Dreamstime
21; PacoRomero/iStock 22-23; Flashgun/cultura/Corbis 25;
Daniel Prudek/iStock 26; Brad Wrobleski/Masterfile/Corbis
29

Printed in the United States of America.

HC 10 9 8 7 6 5 4 3 2 1
PB 10 9 8 7 6 5 4 3 2 1

Table of Contents

Let's Go Rock Climbing

Your fingertips cling to the rock face. Your rope is strung through an anchor at the top of the cliff. The **harness** holds you tight. You set your feet. You call, "Climbing!" Your partner calls back, "Climb!" Then you reach for a higher handhold. It's a great day to go rock climbing!

Climbing is a fun way to
experience the great outdoors.

Scaling rocks is harder than climbing stairs. Climbers are fit athletes.

 Why do I need strong lungs to climb?

Rock climbing is a fun sport. But scaling walls and rock faces is hard work. Climbers need to be in good physical shape. Strong hands will give a sturdy grip. A strong heart and lungs will keep them going. Strong arms and legs will carry them to the top.

 Your muscles need oxygen. If they don't get oxygen, they don't work. Strong lungs help you get as much oxygen as you can.

Climbing Gear

What gear do climbers need? First, they need a pair of climbing shoes. Climbing shoes are flexible. They let the climber bend the foot to get the best foothold. The shoes have soft soles with good grip. Climbers use their climbing shoes only for climbing. Hiking in them wears out the soles.

Climbing shoes are rounded and able to grip uneven surfaces.

Anchors and carabiners hold the ropes in place during a climb.

 Why are springy ropes better for a fall?

A harness and ropes are important for most types of climbing. These will catch a climber in case of a fall. Climbers wear a harness around their legs and hips, like a seat. Ropes connect to the harness with clips called **carabiners**. Climbers often use **dynamic ropes**. These springy ropes help take in the energy of a fall.

 A springy rope will bounce back up a little and lessen the force at the end of the rope.

Types of Climbing

There are lots of ways to climb. Most climbers start with **top-roping**. A rope is looped through an anchor at the top of the wall. The climber attaches one end of the rope to his harness. On the ground, the **belayer** feeds the other end through a **belay device** on her harness. The belayer helps stop the rope to catch a climber in case of a fall.

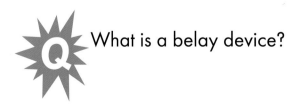 What is a belay device?

The belay device on this woman's harness helps control her partner's rope in case of a fall.

 It is like a brake that stops the rope from moving. It helps the belayer catch a falling climber.

Bouldering is a type of climbing that requires little equipment.

 **Q** Do people climb on snow or ice?

Lead climbing is a challenging type of climbing. There is no anchor at the top of the rock face. One person climbs and places anchors along the route. The other person belays.

Bouldering is a way to scale large rocks. Boulder climbers drop a soft crash pad on the ground. They don't use ropes. If they fall, they get up and try again.

 Yes! Ice climbing is an exciting sport. You'll need spikes attached to your boots or shoes. You also need an ice axe to create holds.

Safety First

Climbing is thrilling. It's also dangerous. Even careful climbers might get badly hurt. Safety comes first. Climb in groups. Tell others where you are climbing and when you'll be back. Check your gear before you leave. Make sure everything is in good condition.

Checking your gear can help prevent climbing accidents.

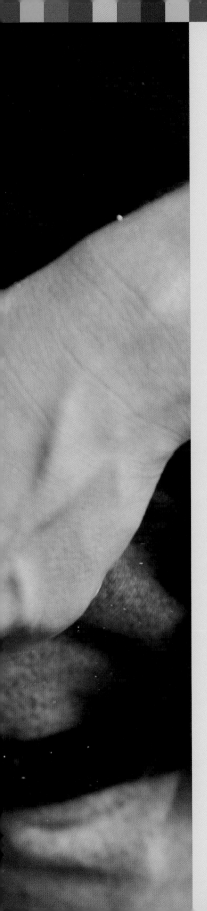

Falls can happen. Wear a helmet to protect your head. To prevent falls, you may want a chalk bag and chalk. Chalk keeps your hands dry. This gives you the best grip on the rock.

Keep an eye on the weather. Dress to keep warm or stay cool. You might want to wear layers of clothing.

A climber rubs chalk on his hands to keep them dry.

A good teammate helps keep everyone safe. When belaying, give your full attention to your climber. When climbing, try not to drop anything. If you do, shout "Rock!" This warns people below you. If you hear someone shout "Rock," keep your head down. Don't look up!

 What do I do if I get scared while climbing?

Never climb alone. A partner can help you in an emergency.

 Tell your belayer that you need a break. Try to relax. Take some deep breaths.

Where to Go

Don't just go out to a mountain to start climbing! You need practice first. It's best to start in a climbing gym. Take a class. Learn the right way to climb and belay. Master the basics. Get familiar with your gear and how it works.

A beginning climber practices on a rock wall.

Soon you'll be ready to leave the gym. Start out small. Master some simple climbs at first. You might join a climbing club. More experienced climbers will help get you on your way. Some gyms and climbing clubs offer trips. Sign up for one to climb with a guide.

 How do I know how hard a climb is?

A climbing guide gives expert advice to a young climber.

 Popular climbs have route ratings. Most mountain routes are rated 5.1 through 5.15. The higher the number, the harder the climb.

Mt. Everest, the tallest mountain in the world, is one of the toughest to climb.

 Which peaks make up the Seven Summits?

You can take on bigger and harder climbs as you get better. You may one day be ready for the world's toughest climbs. Many of the world's top climbers scale the Seven Summits. These are the tallest mountains on each of the seven continents.

 The Seven Summits are Mt. Everest, Cerro Aconcagua, Denali, Mt. Kilimanjaro, Mt. Elbrus, Vinson Massif, and Carstensz Pyramid.

Rock climbing takes some hard work and learning. But most climbers agree that it's worth it. There's nothing like looking down at a rock face you have climbed. So grab a harness, step into your shoes, and get climbing!

Have patience. The challenges of rock climbing provide a sense of accomplishment.

Glossary

belay device A brake for a climbing rope that helps the belayer control a climber's fall.

belayer A person who secures another climber by controlling his or her rope.

bouldering A type of climbing that is done near to the ground and without a rope.

carabiner A type of clip that climbers use to connect their ropes to their harnesses.

dynamic rope A climbing rope that has elasticity, or springiness, built into it to absorb the energy of a fall.

harness A piece of gear that fits around your legs and waist and connects a climber to a rope.

lead climbing A type of climbing in which climbers attach anchors as they scale a rock face and take turns belaying for each other.

top-roping A type of climbing in which an anchor is set at the top of a rock face and a belayer stays on the ground.

Read More

Doeden, Matt. *Can You Survive Extreme Mountain Climbing?: An Interactive Survival Adventure.* North Mankato, Minn.: Capstone Press, 2013.

Green, Sara. *Mountain Climbing.* Minneapolis: Bellwether Media, Inc., 2013.

Tomljanovic, Tatiana. *Rock Climbing.* New York: AV2 by Weigl, 2014.

Websites

Climbing Magazine
http://www.climbing.com/

How Rock Climbing Works
http://adventure.howstuffworks.com/outdoor-activities/climbing/rock-climbing.htm

PBS Kids—Dragonfly TV: Rock Climbing
http://pbskids.org/dragonflytv/show/rockclimbing.html

Index

About the Author

Author and editor Matt Doeden has written
hundreds of children's and young adult books.
Several of his titles have been Junior Library
Guild selections and listed among the Best
Children's Books of the Year by the Children's
Book Committee at Bank Street College.
Doeden, a recreational climber, lives in
Minnesota with his wife and two children.